A CENTURY OF
ROYALTY

Published in Great Britain in 2014 by Shire Publications Ltd, PO Box 883, Oxford, OX1 9PL, UK.

PO Box 3985, New York, NY 10185-3985, USA.

E-mail: shire@shirebooks.co.uk   www.shirebooks.co.uk

A CIP catalogue record for this book is available from the British Library.

Shire Century No.1.   ISBN-13: 978 0 74781 273 9

Ed West has asserted his right under the Copyright, Designs and Patents Act, 1988, to be identified as the author of this book.

Designed by S. Larking and typeset in Swiss 721.

Printed in China through Worldprint Ltd.

14 15 16 17 18   10 9 8 7 6 5 4 3 2 1

A CENTURY OF
ROYALTY

ED WEST

CONTENTS

INTRODUCTION

In 1917, towards the end of the First World War, the House of Windsor was born by royal proclamation with George V's decision to change the family name from the Germanic Saxe-Coburg-Gotha. In many ways this marked the beginning of the age of modern royalty, responding as it did to popular pressure for the royals to disassociate themselves from Britain's German enemy.

Living through the overthrow of the Austro-Hungarian Habsburgs, the German Hohenzollerns, and the murder of Russia's Romanovs, George V would create in Britain a modern, adaptable royal family for the twentieth century. Unlike his royal cousins, George would survive as king after the epoch-ending First World War to thrive in a new world.

To his granddaughter Lilibet (the future Queen Elizabeth II) he was 'Grandpa England', but with the skilful use of new technology such as radio broadcasts, he would become a father figure for the nation and the Commonwealth. This idea of a new type of royalty continued under his son George VI, who in key respects transformed the royals into a middle-class family with whom the nation could identify, and helped to hold the country together during the traumas and disruption of the Second World War.

From the first days of modern mass communication to the wedding of the Duke and Duchess of Cambridge and the Diamond Jubilee, the royal family has been many things: a national soap opera, with its very own dark moments; a slice of Ruritania in a world of presidents, democracies and dictatorships; a social institution; and an essential part of national identity.

Under Queen Elizabeth II royalty has continued to adapt to the modern world, and despite some bad times, remains the strongest of British institutions. And from the photographs of the funeral of Edward VII, which captured the quaint sight of kings in his cortege who would soon find themselves at war, to the age of Facebook updates for the British Monarchy's 620,000 online fans, it is a story told on camera.

Their history is also the most visible and well known of modern Britain, taking in the instability and horror of the First World War, the difficult inter-war period and the life-or-death struggle against Nazism, the social changes of the 1960s and the country's attempts to find a new place in the twenty-first century. *A Century of Royalty* captures the major events that have shaped modern Britain, as well as the glamour of royalty, an almost magical force exemplified *in extremis* by Princess Diana. It illustrates the enormous psychological impact that the royal family (and its individual members) has had on people's lives, sometimes struggling, but mostly succeeding, in its very public role. Despite the troubles of the 1990s (and of Edward VIII's abdication) it is the story of the ultimate survivors throughout one hundred years of British history right through to the latest generation and the happy arrival in July 2013 of another royal George.

Edward VII's Funeral

In many ways the story of the twentieth century begins with the funeral of Edward VII, the last British king to bear a German surname (and because of his heavily Germanic upbringing, a slight accent). For all the glamour and technological buzz of the Edwardian era – the age of the Wright Brothers, Thomas Edison, radio and cinema – it was now a distant world of traditional monarchs.

Nine kings and thirty-two princes would follow the coffin of Edward, a popular, jovial figure with a great lust for life (and women and food), whose greatest legacy was the use of royalty as a force for diplomacy. Famously charming and graceful, he arrived in Paris in 1904 to a hostile crowd and left them shouting '*vive le roi!*' Alas, Anglo-French *rapprochement* went in tandem with growing unease at the ambitions of Germany, led by the king's undiplomatic and socially inept nephew, Kaiser Wilhelm II.

As Edward's coffin travelled from Buckingham Palace to Westminster Hall, up Whitehall and the Mall to Marble Arch and Paddington, and by train to Windsor, the king-emperor was mourned by monarchs and princes from across the globe, including representatives from Russia, Germany and Austria-Hungary, in the latter case Archduke Franz Ferdinand.

George V and Kaiser Wilhelm II

Of the four great European monarchies of the year that Franz Ferdinand's assassination sparked a world war, only the British House of Saxe-Coburg-Gotha would survive, remoulded for the new age.

Just a year before this, King George V visited his cousin Wilhelm in Berlin and was photographed with him, wearing the uniform of the Prussian Food Guards. George V was an honorary officer in the German regiment, much to the disgust of his Danish mother Queen Alexandra, who was still resentful about her country's 1864 war with Prussia (the Second Schleswig War, famously the most obscure conflict in history, understood by 'only three people, one of them mad'). Kaiser Wilhelm, the son of Queen Victoria's eldest child Vicky, had a difficult relationship with Britain, and an inferiority complex. He favoured a more expansionist Germany, but lacked the diplomatic cunning of his grandfather's chancellor Otto Von Bismarck, once unnerving the king of Belgium at a dinner by telling him that he could have a chunk of France in return for military support. It could have been very different; Wilhelm's father, Kaiser Friedrich III was a reforming Anglophile who wanted to install a more British-style parliamentary democracy in Berlin, but tragically he died young of cancer. In this photograph, a family similarity can be seen between the king and the kaiser but George had an even closer and even more remarkable physical resemblance.

The First World War

On 1 July 1916 the British launched the offensive that would come to define our view of the First World War – the Battle of the Somme. Twenty thousand British soldiers were killed in one day, another 40,000 wounded, and General Haig's reputation would go into freefall as the century went on. George V and Haig are pictured here on either side of the French General Ferdinand Foch on the terrace of Haig's headquarters in Beauquesne, France.

The king had been a rallying point for the British forces, and his wife, Queen Mary of Teck, spent much of the war visiting wounded and dying servicemen, which she found an emotional strain. As the fighting went on, the royal family became increasingly concerned about whether it might survive, and on 27 June 1917 King George changed the family name to Windsor, relinquishing all the German titles held by the family, and stripping fifteen German relatives of British titles.

The spur was the abdication of his cousin, Tsar Nicholas II, and the fear of revolution spreading to England. But it was also unfortunate that from 1916 London was bombed by German aircraft, the most famous of which, the Gotha G.IV, sounded uncomfortably similar to George's and the royal family's name. The Bolsheviks murdered Tsar Nicholas, his wife and five children, while the kaiser ended up exiled to the Netherlands where he died in 1940.

The Prince of Wales Visiting Curran Munitions Works, Cardiff

Prince Edward, known to his family as David (his seventh Christian name), was twenty when the war began, and joined the Grenadier Guards, but Lord Kitchener had refused him a place at the front line, fearing the loss to morale if he was captured or killed. Despite this he did see trench warfare and won the Military Cross in 1916, earning him the respect of other soldiers, for whom class privileges counted for less than the ability to fight with courage and not 'funk'.

Although the prince would later become something of a dissolute playboy, in his early twenties he took a keen interest in the conditions of the poor, touring the most run down parts of the country. He famously said 'something must be done' after a visit to South Wales.

It was also necessary for the royals to appear to care; by the end of the war Britain faced numerous threats in the form of Communism, Irish republicanism and increasing unrest in the colonies, while in Germany political instability was caused by the return of demobbed soldiers. Having failed to give asylum to the Romanovs, the Royal Navy was sent, however, to rescue the Greek royals (including an infant, later to become Prince Philip).

King George V Tries Bricklaying

George's reign began with the 1911 Parliament Act crisis, the last ever serious dispute between Parliament's houses of Commons and Lords, at a time when growing trade-union militancy made it appear that Britain was coming close to class warfare.

There was a conscious effort to make the royal family more broad-based and to win the support of the working classes, which the king found uncomfortable at first, but proved unquestionably successful. The British Labour Movement, which may well have grown republican, became broadly pro-monarchy, and George in particular developed a good relationship with the leadership of the moderate-socialist Labour Party, which first came to power in the 1920s.

After the war the Government Instructional Factory (right) for ex-servicemen was set up in Cricklewood by the Ministry of Labour, but the government's perceived inaction in helping the wounded had led to much bitterness (and changed public opinion of the war).

During the General Strike of 1926 the king urged the government to be moderate and objected to strikers being called 'revolutionaries', saying 'Try living on their wages before you judge them.' He also encouraged the formation of a national government in 1931 and volunteered to reduce the cost of the civil list.

The Young Princes

Born eighteen months apart and raised together, the diminutive princes (Edward was only 5 feet 7 inches, Albert 5 feet 8 inches) were polar opposites in character. Edward was athletic and confident; Bertie (as he was known to the family) was painfully shy and a slow learner. The pair were 'a cock pheasant [and] an ugly duckling' in the words of one contemporary.

In the 1920s Prince Edward was, to use a later phrase, a style icon; among the many innovations he popularised were the Windsor knot, the wearing of sweaters and berets rather than frock coats at informal events, plus fours, and dinner jackets in the evening. During that decade, as people turned to hedonism to drown out the horror of the First World War, Edward's style was a reaction to the more conservative formality of his father, but it also reflected the lifestyle of the new aristocrats – a world of parties, sports and flying from one fashionable spot to the next.

He was not the first royal trendsetter. At his death in 1830 George IV's wardrobe was worth the equivalent of £1.2millon and Edward VII, another playboy, also influenced men's fashion. In this picture the two princes (centre and centre right) are heading to a rugby match between Wales and Ireland at Cardiff Arms Park.

Arrival of Princess Elizabeth

Elizabeth Bowes-Lyon, the youngest daughter of the Earl of Strathmore and Kinghorne (right of Prince Albert), was raised in Glamis, a Scottish castle which was used as a hospital for wounded soldiers in the war, while four of her brothers fought at the front (only three came back). Bertie asked Elizabeth three times to become his bride, the first time the poor prince being so cripplingly shy that he used a go-between; fearful of becoming a royal, she nevertheless came to love him. Alongside the parents are George V, Queen Mary and other family members. Elizabeth was born on 21 April with this formal family photograph being taken less than a week later.

Princess Elizabeth with Grandparents

George V enjoyed a warm relationship with his granddaughters, while Queen Mary often took them on trips to art galleries and museums.

Mostly of German stock, Queen Mary's father was a financially hopeless minor royal who had been relegated to the title of Serene Highness because of his low-ranking marriage, was constantly in debt and relied on parliamentary subsidy. It was largely due to her godmother Queen Victoria's fondness for young Mary that she was betrothed to the second in line to the throne, Prince Albert, but this piece of good fortune turned sour when a short time into the engagement he died in the great flu epidemic of the 1890s (along with a million others). While in mourning she had grown close to Albert's brother George and in 1893 he proposed.

Theirs was a love match, and unlike his father, George never had a mistress. Although he could be a frightening father, she was a loving if somewhat stern mother; when in 1901 George and Mary had gone on the first royal tour of the empire, she cried at the prospect of having to leave their three children (the youngest was just a year old).

George V's Funeral

The world George V left was vastly different to the one in which he had grown up. When he was just fourteen he had been sent away to sea and crossed the Pacific Ocean (where he had a dragon tattoo done) shortly after his grandmother had assumed the title of Empress of India. By the 1930s the political landscape had transformed, the Indian independence movement was gathering strength, and the British Empire was already well on its way to decline. George V had a difficult relationship with his four surviving sons, who at his death held the 'Vigil of the Princes', standing guard over their father's body as it lay in state (the Queen Mother's four grandsons would do the same in 2002).

George's youngest surviving son, George, Duke of Kent, was a talented pianist and dancer who had been forced into the Navy, and went off the rails, drinking heavily, using opium and partying with the decadent white highlands set in Kenya. It took his brother Edward, of all people, to talk sense into him, and he married a Greek princess and joined the civil service, although he is said to have had a number of affairs, one of them with the notorious Duchess of Argyll. His children, the Duke of Kent and Prince Michael of Kent, are still prominent members of the royal family.

Abdication Crisis

'After I am dead', George V had said of his heir, 'the boy will ruin himself in twelve months'. The prince's high living had been a concern since the late 1920s, but in truth he never felt comfortable being king and had spoken about renouncing his position even before he met Wallis Simpson.

Edward was introduced to Wallis Simpson, already divorced *and* re-married, through his mistress, Thelma Furness, in 1931. Special Branch operatives described him as being 'under her thumb', and ministers were also reluctant to send confidential papers to the king, as he took little interest and they were concerned that Simpson might see them. In August the king and Wallis went away on a cruise, and by October it was clear that he intended to marry her. Public opinion was divided, but the consensus in the establishment was that marriage to the American socialite could not be countenanced.

The abdication declared on 10 December 1936 would throw his nervous brother Bertie into 'the void', as the latter called it. Born in 1895, Bertie suffered from ill health, was cruelly treated by his nanny and floundered academically. Although he spent five years in the Navy, he had to be sent home from the war with appendicitis. This picture of George in the back of a car seems to capture much of the reluctance and dread of a man who never wanted to be king.

People Queue for Abdication Speech Recording

In 1924 King George V had made his first radio broadcast to 10 million people and in 1932 he had instituted the Christmas radio address (the first television address was in 1957 and the first 3D one came in 2012). As Prince of Wales, Edward was enthusiastic about the new technology and made fifty broadcasts, and it was the medium he would use to announce the shattering news of his abdication.

Edward and Simpson had been on a cruise in the Mediterranean over the late summer and by the end of October the scandal was breaking. Although the affair had only been reported in the foreign press, most people in Britain were unaware until later despite letters from family abroad that were fuelling rumours.

The British newspapers remained silent, and the BBC was especially criticised for ignoring the constitutional crisis until days before the abdication.

It broke by accident after the Bishop of Bradford gave a sermon on the king's 'need for grace'. The press took it as a green light to report on the king's intention to marry, although it later transpired that the bishop had never heard of Simpson and was talking about something else.

Awaiting the Coronation

In the words of one Labour MP, the abdication crisis did 'more for republicanism than fifty years of propaganda', and George VI lamented that he assumed 'a rocking throne'. Spain had recently become the latest country to abolish its monarchy, and George, who cried on his mother's shoulder upon being told he must be king, had an enormous task in steadying his crown. His concern was shared by officials, who had drafted a report into his fitness to rule and who had considered a scheme where the throne was passed to one of his younger brothers (neither of whom were especially fit for the job either).

But George stepped into the breach, his face was painted over Edward's on the official coronation portrait, and the ceremony showed the power that the monarchy still had over people's hearts, even if there were several mishaps, such as the Dean of Westminster fumbling the oath. Interest in the monarch was intense and, as the picture opposite shows, crowds lined the streets readying themselves to observe the spectacle.

Although the 1953 coronation is remembered as the great television event, George's coronation was in fact watched by around 10,000 people at home on the BBC's new high-definition television service begun in 1936 – the first outside broadcast. Edward's face had been the BBC's first testcard.

The King and Queen Visit the Poor

Like many aristocrats who had fought in the First World War alongside the ranks, the king, when Duke of York, had developed a great sense of guilt towards the poor, and during his father's reign his great mission was the Duke's camps, where boys from different social backgrounds spent summers together and mingled. After the Great Depression began in 1929 80 per cent of children in the mining areas of County Durham and the poorest areas of London showed signs of rickets, and half of people in economically depressed areas did not have enough food to live healthily. There was fear of unrest. Communism and Fascism were spreading across Europe, and a BBC series charting unemployment was considered so explosive that the Labour government told Lord Reith in 1934 to take it off air. He refused. This picture shows the king and queen at Tow Law Social Service Centre, surrounded by crowds. Fewer than nine months later Britain was at war with Germany and the royals and the nation faced yet greater challenges.

The Duke and Duchess of Windsor in Wartime Uniform

Edward and Wallis Simpson were married in France in 1937, and made an ill-advised tour of Germany, where they met Adolf Hitler. Having settled in the south of France, Edward was assigned to the British Expeditionary Force, but fearful of his possible Nazi sympathies, the government had him sent to the Bahamas as governor until 1945; perhaps not the worst place on earth to be during those years, but the couple remained outcasts, Edward dying in 1972 and Simpson in 1986.

Despite their politics, Simpson's American husband Ernest was Jewish, revered the monarchy and Britain, and behaved like a perfect gentleman during the divorce, causing minimal scandal. The abdication had led to the complete collapse of the brothers' relationship. They had begun to drift apart in their twenties, especially after the arrival of Elizabeth Bowes-Lyon, a more forceful character than her husband who disapproved of her brother-in-law's lifestyle and also hated the way that Edward teased his younger brother for his stammer.

After the wedding the king declined to allow the couple to return to England, Simpson was not granted the title 'Her Royal Highness', and even Edward's closest brother, the Duke of Kent, refused to be his best man.

King George and Elizabeth Visit Sheffield

Although it was Winston Churchill who became the symbol of national resistance during the Battle of Britain, the king and queen were vital for morale during the country's darkest hour. Hitler called Queen Elizabeth 'the most dangerous woman in Europe'.

Like many, the king privately feared that London would be devastated and that Nazi conquest was inevitable, but he intended to go down fighting, and was seen practising with his revolver at Buckingham Palace after the Luftwaffe assault began. The king and queen were urged to send their daughters to Canada or Australia, but they refused to go without their mother, and she without her husband. Queen Mary was evacuated to Badminton House in Gloucestershire along with fifty-five staff and seventy pieces of luggage, and would often give lifts to soldiers walking down the road, much to their astonishment.

As the country was blitzed, with 40,000 killed in German raids, Buckingham Palace itself took a hit, leading the king to reflect that they 'could look the East End in the face' now that they had suffered the terror. Indeed, the family did share in the sacrifice; the Duke of Kent was killed in 1942 while on a mission to Iceland. In this photograph taken in Sheffield, which had suffered greatly from German attacks, the royals encounter some of those people made homeless in the raids, and their presence and compassion on such occasions undoubtedly added to the monarch's popularity.

Elizabeth the Mechanic

Churchill once said of the future queen that she had an 'air of authority and reflectiveness astonishing in an infant'. The two princesses spent the war in Sandringham, Balmoral and Windsor, where they staged pantomimes in aid of raising money for wool.

In 1940, aged fourteen, Elizabeth made her first radio broadcast, addressing other children for the BBC's 'Children's Hour' and telling them that 'We are trying to do all we can to help our gallant sailors, soldiers and airmen, and we are trying, too, to bear our share of the danger and sadness of war. We know, every one of us, that in the end all will be well'.

Just before she turned nineteen, Princess Elizabeth joined the Auxiliary Territorial Service and spent six months in Aldershot learning to be a driver and mechanic, and how to strip an engine. Rather unusually for a mechanic, she was already counsellor of state, giving her powers in the absence of her father abroad.

She made her first overseas tour to Africa in 1947, where on her twenty-first birthday she addressed the Commonwealth, declaring that her whole life 'shall be devoted to your service and the service of our great imperial family'.

Prince Philip the Night Before his Wedding

Although the embodiment of the gruff English aristocrat, military in bearing and with a wicked sense of humour (his famous gaffes fill whole volumes), Prince Philip's story is one of reinvention: his first language as a boy was French.

He was born in Corfu in 1921 to the Greek royal family, which lost everything following defeat in the Greco-Turkish war and struggled as exiles. His mother, Princess Alice of Battenberg, deaf and later schizophrenic, ended up running away to become a Greek Orthodox nun, as well as being honoured as one of the 'Righteous Among the Nations' for her role saving Jews in the war.

Philip fled Germany in 1933 and came under the care of his uncle, Louis Mountbatten holding the cigar, who brought together the handsome young mid-shipman and the Princess. Only Queen Mary was suspicious of the newcomer, referring to him as 'the Hun', despite her own not entirely British origins.

It was indeed thought that Philip's family name, Schleswig-Holstein-Sonderburg-Glücksburg, might be a touch too German for the times. Philip changed it to Mountbatten, although Queen Mary persuaded Churchill to insist that the royal family's own should continue as the House of Windsor. Since then, Philip has been a colourful royal consort and a national treasure of sorts, known for his irreverence. This shows him celebrating with naval friends the night before his wedding to the future queen.

The Royal Wedding

The king made Philip 'His Royal Highness' on the day before his wedding to his second cousin (once removed), and on the morning he became the Duke of Edinburgh (a title that Prince Edward will inherit). He also converted from Greek Orthodoxy to Anglicanism.

Having just endured six years of war, with the economy crippled and Britain's cities smashed to pieces, the nation faced hard times of fuel shortages and rations known as the austerity years. In fitting with the spirit of the age, the princess had to buy the material for her gown using coupons.

The couple received over 2,500 wedding presents from around the world and some 10,000 telegrams of congratulation, and although the wedding was attended by foreign royalty, it was one much depleted compared to the days of her great-grandfather's funeral. There were also a number of noted absences; Prince Philip's three sisters, being German, were excluded, as was the Duke of Windsor. The king's sister Mary, in mourning for her husband, excused herself on grounds of sickness, although it was later claimed she did not attend because she was upset at Edward not being invited. Here the couple are seen leaving Westminster Abbey immediately after the wedding.

Prince Charles with Grandfather George VI

Charles was born in 1948 – baptised by the Archbishop of Canterbury with water from the River Jordan – followed by Anne in 1950. By this time the king was gravely ill, having steadied his nerves through smoking, which had led to lung cancer. (Ironically it had been the Nazis, his adversaries in the Second World War, who had discovered the link.)

Even after the war there was much work to do, with the monarch helping the transition from empire to Commonwealth, and it was far from smooth; India gained independence in 1947 and Ireland and South Africa both left the Commonwealth. 'Why leave the family?' the king had pleaded with Irish leaders, even asking if it was something he had done, but too much blood had been spilt since his father's last royal visit to the country in 1911 for the nations to be reconciled. It would not be politically possible for a British monarch to visit the Irish Republic until 2011.

His 1947 tour of South Africa also left a bitter taste. The king, who as a young man had raised eyebrows in the Caribbean by playing mixed doubles tennis with a black man, was disgusted when told he could only shake hands with white men.

George VI Waves Goodbye to His Daughter

By the time of his 1951 Christmas broadcast the king was dying. Despite this, it was decided that Princess Elizabeth should go ahead with her tour of Africa, one of numerous trips she would make to the continent over the coming decades.

On 31 January George was captured on film waving goodbye to his daughter at London airport, the last time they would ever see each other. On 6 February he was found dead in bed at Sandringham, aged just fifty-six. Elizabeth was in the Kenyan bush with Prince Philip when the news came through the wires from England, and it took several hours before a journalist was able to pass the message to one of Elizabeth's equerries, who relayed the news to Philip.

Two days later she was back in England and proclaimed queen. Prayers were said for the king across the country (even down mines, where priests led miners in prayer for his soul), and some 300,000 went to pay their respects as the king's body lay in state. It would be little or no exaggeration to say he had sat on the throne during the country's most difficult days in a millennium.

Three Queens Upon the Death of George VI

Queen Mary (middle) had now outlived three sons and seen another estranged and disgraced. The Queen Mother (right), as she was now titled to avoid confusion with her daughter of the same name, initially retired to Scotland, devastated by the loss of her husband. It was only after a meeting with Churchill that she returned to public duties, which she performed for the next fifty years. After Charles had asked his grandmother whether grandpa would come back, she hugged her grandson and he told her: 'Don't cry, Granny.'

Crowds had gathered first thing that bitterly cold February morning to line the procession of the funeral, and to pay tribute to a man her widow described as 'my dear husband, a great and noble king'. She said to them: 'I commend to you our dear daughter: give her your loyalty and devotion in the great and lonely station to which she has been called. She will need your protection and love.'

The queen (rear) was lucky to have in Churchill a wise and avuncular prime minister, just as Queen Victoria had the elderly Lord Melbourne to guide her through her terrifying first moments as monarch.

The Coronation

Coronations are held some time after the preceding monarch's death, in order to allow a suitable period for mourning, and although Queen Mary had died just weeks before the June event, she had stated in her will that she wished it to go ahead as planned.

Fashion designer Norman Hartnell tried nine different designs for the queen's dress before they were both satisfied with the white silk gown embroidered with flowers representing the four home nations and seven Commonwealth countries. The designer also included, without her knowledge, a four-leaf clover on the left side, for luck.

The queen prepared for the big day by wearing the Imperial State Crown wherever she went, which is 12 inches tall and includes 2,868 diamonds, 273 pearls and eleven emeralds, and a sapphire that was part of Edward the Confessor's crown in the eleventh century. The coronation ceremony itself is truly ancient, and some of the ritual bears a resemblance to the first such coronation, held by Elizabeth's direct ancestor King Edgar in 973.

During the ceremony Prince Philip (kneeling in the picture) pledged to be her 'liege man of life and limb'.

The Coronation: a Street Party

The coronation was an important milestone in broadcasting history, as the first national television event – twenty million watched the ceremony, at a time when there were just two million television sets in Britain, gathering around to listen to Richard Dimbleby's commentary and watch the young queen. Outside street parties across Britain, like this one in Pinnington Road, Gorton North, Manchester, celebrated the event in their own way.

During the day jet bombers flew footage to Canada, where it was broadcast to the United States. Prime Minister Winston Churchill had not wanted cameras at such a mystical event, but had lost the vote in the Commons, with supporters arguing that the queen wished her subjects to see her. The Church was also broadly in favour.

One part was not televised: when the queen sat in the Coronation Chair and the Archbishop of Canterbury anointed her with holy oil from the same container as the one used to anoint her father. This was considered sacrosanct, and so was concealed from the television cameras by a silk canopy held above the queen by four knights of the garter.

Ava Gardner Meets the Queen

Since the age of cinema, radio and television began, royals have enjoyed (if that is the word) the same level of fame as film stars, and the two have often rubbed shoulders. In the mid-1950s Ava Gardner was at the height of her fame, at this point being married to Frank Sinatra, whom she had stolen from his wife Nancy in the femme fatale style. The sultry Hollywood actress had recently starred in what most consider her finest role, in *The Barefoot Contessa* (1954) alongside Humphrey Bogart.

The queen has met countless film stars down the years, from Marilyn Monroe to Daniel Craig, with whom she starred in the opening ceremony to the 2012 Olympics, despite being advised against it. The head of British Film and Television Awards (BAFTA) called her 'the most memorable Bond girl yet'. The royal endorsement of film has a more important side, being as it is part of the new royal remit to promote British industry. In 2013 Her Majesty was awarded a 'BAFTA' for her lifetime of support for British film and television, Kenneth Branagh presenting the award.

Princess Margaret with the Beatles

Still a fairly clean-cut group of young lads from Liverpool, the Beatles' performance in November 1963 at the Prince of Wales Theatre (in a gala that included Marlene Dietrich) captivated both Princess Margaret and (rather more surprisingly) the Queen Mother.

The queen's beautiful younger sister was hit hard by her father's death and soon after fell in love with Captain Peter Townsend, an older man who was divorced and a commoner, and so unsuitable. Instead she married the aristocratic fashion photographer Antony Armstrong-Jones, who turned out to be just as inappropriate, a notorious womaniser who fathered a love child during their marriage. Always the more glamorous of the sisters, Margaret hung around a racy crowd in the 1960s, sometimes to the concern of the authorities, but her marriage collapsed rather swiftly and unpleasantly when pictures of her with one Roddy Llewellyn (many years her junior) on a Caribbean beach in 1976 reached the tabloids. Lord Snowdon, as Armstrong-Jones became, never changed – his second marriage ended in 2000 when it was revealed he had fathered another child (outside wedlock), at the age of sixty-seven. Margaret was gradually to retreat from public life.

Margaret and Snowdon attended at least two more Beatles concerts, although Lennon handed back the MBE he received from the queen, in protest against British support for the Nigerian government in its civil war with Biafran rebels.

Bobby Moore Introduces the Queen to the England Team

It was perhaps one of the most famous moments of the queen's reign, and one that captured the excitement of London in the 1960s. At the 1966 World Cup the queen attended the first game – England v Uruguay (pictured) – where Bobby Moore first introduced her to England's most famous line-up. She would later present Moore with the trophy after his team had beaten West Germany 4-2.

The queen first performed this role back in 1949 when, as Princess Elizabeth, she handed the FA Cup to Billy Wright, captain of Wolverhampton Wanderers, but it was George V and George VI who regularly presided at major football and rugby matches. (During the 1914 Five Nations contest George V would hand the trophy to an England rugby team, six of whom would soon die in the First World War.)

As the queen is rather more of a horse-racing fan, other sporting events have been left to other members of the royal family, such as the Duchess of Kent, who until the late 2000s presented Wimbledon tennis championship medals, and famously consoled the defeated, crying Jana Novotna in 1993 with a maternal arm around the shoulder (they remained good friends afterwards).

The Aberfan Disaster

The queen and Prince Philip looked visibly shocked as they visited the small Welsh village of Aberfan just eight days after the most horrific tragedy of modern British history. Monarchs, like modern US presidents, are expected to offer solace at the scene of major disasters, such obligations representing one of royalty's most affecting responsibilities.

As far back as 1963 concerns had been raised about the debris that had been piled up by the National Coal Board above the village. But on 21 October 1966 more than 150,000 cubic metres of earth slid down the hill and into the side of Pantglas Junior School, where the children were leaving assembly on the last day before half term – moments later 116 children and twenty-seven adults were dead. The twenty-eight survivors in the school recall a tremendous aeroplane-like noise, blackness and then a deathly silence. Most victims died from asphyxiation.

When the queen arrived she received a posy from a three-year-old girl with the words: 'From the remaining children of Aberfan'. Onlookers described her as being on the verge of tears.

During her 2012 Jubilee she would revisit the village to open a new school, her fifth visit since the tragedy. The original school has since been demolished and turned into a memorial gardens and the mine has gone, but the villagers have struggled to get on with their lives.

The Family at Windsor Castle

After a long break Philip and Elizabeth had two more children; Andrew (right), born in 1960, was the first child born to a reigning monarch since Princess Beatrice in 1857, and he was followed by Edward (left) in 1964. At the time of this portrait Charles was at Trinity College, Cambridge, having followed his father by attending Gordonstoun, the rather Spartan Highland school which he hated and called 'Colditz in kilts'. The queen and duke's marriage has always been strong, but their parenting style has had its critics – Charles in particular having a difficult relationship with Philip – although almost every male heir to the throne has had a problem with his father.

Just a year later the royals commissioned a documentary, *The Royal Family*, the idea of which was to show the public that they were just like them. Although the programme attracted extremely high ratings – some two thirds of people saw some of it – it was never shown again, supposedly because the family (and some of the public) had come to think that it took away some of their traditional majesty and mystery. Indeed, many saw it as the start of the disastrous decline in the royals' prestige at the end of the twentieth century.

Charles Becomes Prince of Wales

The role of Prince of Wales says much about the evolution of the British monarchy from brute force to pageantry and ritual. The future Edward II was made the first English Prince of Wales in 1302 after the country was conquered when its prince, Llywelyn the Last, was defeated at the Battle of Orewin Bridge. Edward I sent Llywelyn's head off to London to be crowned in mockery of the Welsh prophecy that a Welshman would be crowned there as king of Britain. Edward also had Llywelyn's only surviving offspring, Gwenllian of Wales, imprisoned, despite her only being six months of age, and she remained incarcerated for the remainder of her life.

The traditional investiture in Caernarfon Castle (birthplace of Edward II) only dates from 1911, and the future Edward VIII hated it. Charles was less resistant, and spent a year in Aberystwyth University beforehand, learning a fair amount of Welsh.

The investiture wasn't entirely welcome – some Welsh nationalists were opposed, and two killed themselves the night before, when the bomb they were planting outside government offices went off. However, support for the monarchy remains strong in Wales, and a poll suggested that the majority of Welsh people would like Prince William to undergo the same ceremony.

Prince Philip and the Queen in Fiji

The queen is head of state to no less than fifteen Commonwealth countries and there is no sign of the appeal of foreign visits diminishing. The year of the Silver Jubilee saw street parties at home and a foreign tour: here the royal couple is presented with a whale tooth. Of all the foreign climes where they have made their mark – she has travelled to 116 countries – Prince Philip has perhaps had the biggest impact in the south Pacific. In nearby Vanatu he is worshipped as a god by the Yaohnanen tribe. The cult emerged in the 1960s, and on learning about it, Philip dutifully sent them a signed photograph. In return they sent him a traditional pig-killing club called a nal-nal.

The Queen's First Grandchild, Peter Phillips

The queen's first grandchild, Anne's son Peter Phillips, was born on 15 November 1977, and seven more grandchildren would follow, the last James, Viscount Severn, in 2007. Because of the now-changed succession law granting precedence to males, James (son to Prince Edward) is now ahead of Peter, but behind Princesses Beatrice and Eugenie. Peter's elder daughter Savannah, born in 2010, was the queen's first great-grandchild.

Princess Anne wanted her children to have relatively normal lives and so she refused the queen's offer of a peerage, making Peter the first legitimate grandchild of a monarch to be born without a title in five hundred years. He has since led a relatively normal life, working in Formula 1 and banking and in 2008 marrying a Canadian, Autumn Kelly, who left the Catholic Church before their marriage. It was announced in 2012 that the law barring royals from marrying Roman Catholics would be changed.

Although very much away from the limelight, Peter Phillips is said to be a supportive cousin to William, five years his junior. Sadly, Anne's marriage would be the first of the new generation's to collapse, when her husband Mark Phillips fathered a child with another woman while they were still married.

Lord Mountbatten's Funeral

A colourful and controversial figure, Louis Mountbatten had risen to the pinnacle of society through charm, wit and a matchmaker's charisma, although question marks hang over his stewardship as last Viceroy of India, where a million lives were lost in the fighting that followed partition. Mountbatten stayed on in Delhi until June 1948, where his last guest was Eamon De Valera, the former IRA leader, who had moved into democratic politics to become Ireland's prime minister.

In 1979 Mountbatten would die at the hands of a new IRA, killed by a bomb placed on his yacht off the coast of Sligo. Two fourteen-year-old boys, one Mountbatten's grandson and the other a local lad, were also killed, in one of the most shocking days of the Troubles (that same day at Warrenpoint, the IRA ambushed and killed eighteen British soldiers). In their loss, the royals had joined the long list of families that had lost a loved one to the Troubles that had begun in 1969.

Lord Mountbatten was given a full military funeral; 118 sailors drew his coffin on a gun carriage to his commemoration service at Westminster Abbey, London. His body was then taken to be buried at Romsey Abbey.

Charles and Diana in Love

For sixteen years the world's foremost celebrity, recognised and adored around the world, fame in the end would become a torture for Diana. She was named after an eighteenth-century relative, Lady Diana Spencer, who died of tuberculosis at the age of twenty-four, and her namesake's life was similarly tragic. Her parents separated when she was eight and, after a bitter custody battle in which her maternal grandmother sided with her son-in-law against her own daughter, she was raised by the Earl.

Charles and Diana had first met in 1977, when he was dating her older sister, Sarah, and the future princess was attending a finishing school. It was not until the summer of 1980, when they were both guests at Balmoral, that he began to take an interest, and he proposed in February 1981. Charles was under pressure to marry, and he had found a suitably pure, innocent and beautiful English girl of good stock. It turned out to be a terrible match, yet nevertheless they did appear to be in love, 'whatever love means', as Charles rather ominously said.

The engagement was announced in February 1981, with Diana selecting a £30,000 ring of fourteen solitaire diamonds surrounding a twelve-carat Ceylon sapphire with eighteen-carat white gold. It must have seemed like a fairytale.

The Queen Laughing, with Charles and Diana

Marrying into 'the Firm', as Philip called it, would prove too much for Diana, but for many years she represented an enormous asset, and possessed an unlimited capacity for putting people at ease, such as here with family at the Highland Games. Noted more for her sober dignity, the queen's lively sense of humour that insiders frequently report is captured in this rare shot.

As well as being popular at home, Diana also spent much of the 1980s on a world charm offensive that left few places unconquered – her first trip to the Netherlands in 1982 was followed by trips to Australia, New Zealand and Canada in 1983, Italy in 1985 (where they met Pope John Paul II) and later that year the US, where the Princess was an enormous hit. Even the Saudis eased their strict rule about the separation of the sexes by inviting her to King Fawd's palace.

Wherever she went, the former nursery teacher took an interest in the young, visiting disabled children in Kuwait and Aids orphans in Africa.

Her first solo overseas official visit was in September 1982 when she represented the queen at the funeral of Princess Grace of Monaco, who had died in a car crash, and with whom she had been compared – alas, history was to repeat itself.

Prince Andrew Returns from the Falklands

Prince Andrew had gone straight from school to the Navy, becoming a helicopter pilot at nineteen, and his ship, HMS *Invincible*, played a major part in the recapture of the Falklands after the Argentinian invasion of April 1982.

Although the government had recommended that he be moved to desk duties, the queen refused, and the prince served as a helicopter pilot on board the ship, taking part in missile decoy and search-and-air rescue, among other dangerous tasks; he was one of the first to take off survivors from the SS *Atlantic Conveyor*. Before it was overthrown by a democratic revolt, the Argentinian junta planned on assassinating the prince in the summer, but did not go through with it. The *Invincible*, along with the rest of the convoy, received a jubilant reception upon arriving in Portsmouth.

Praised for his skills as a pilot and officer, he was decorated and remained active in the Navy until 2001, and every year he lays a wreath for the Falklands dead at the annual Remembrance Day ceremony in London. After leaving active service, he became the United Kingdom's Special Representative for International Trade and Investment, promoting British business to foreign investors.

Charles, Diana and William

William was born in June and baptised on the Queen Mother's 82nd birthday by the Archbishop of Canterbury. Due to become the fifth monarch to be so called, he was named after Charles's childhood friend and cousin Prince William of Gloucester, who was killed in 1972 in an air crash, aged just thirty.

'Wombat', as William was called by his parents (the nickname Wills was in fact first thought up by the press), was taken on a royal tour to Australia when he was just a baby, which struck the right note with the public, although it later transpired that it was only at the suggestion of the Australian prime minister.

Keen to make her children aware of how other people lived, Diana took them to hamburger chain McDonald's and let them play with the sort of toys that normal children might have, such as video games. From a fairly early age she introduced them to the charities she worked with, and their early experience of meeting Aids orphans and others less fortunate has certainly shaped them.

The Queen with Ronald and Nancy Reagan

During the glory days of Anglo-American relations, the two heads of state shared a passion that transcended politics – horses. Before the visit the president's men fretted over what he should wear riding (no formal attire needed) while the British agonised about what to give the president (deciding on a carriage clock). The tiptoeing had a very serious side – Cold War tensions were at a new height and the British were keen for a show of strength against the Soviet Union.

It was only revealed thirty years later that Reagan had failed to reply to the queen's initial invitation for several weeks, due to organisational failings at the White House, although it was also suggested that Nancy Reagan's fondness for consulting astrologers was the reason.

During that trip in 1982, Reagan also cemented his relationship with Prime Minister Margaret Thatcher and became the first US president to address a meeting of both houses of parliament, telling them that Communism would be 'left on the ash heap of history'. Meanwhile Philip's view of the Soviets was well known. Asked whether he'd wish to visit the USSR in 1967, he said: 'I would like to go to Russia very much – although the bastards murdered half my family.'

This picture records a later visit of the queen to the president's ranch in the Santa Ynez mountains in California.

Charles and Diana with Baby Harry

Although the public was thrilled by the birth of the couple's second son, behind the scenes the marriage was falling apart.

Just a month after the birth Charles would resume his affair with Camilla Parker-Bowles, whom he had given up before the wedding in order to give the marriage a chance, but he had never stopped loving her. It was only afterwards that Diana in turn met Captain James Hewitt.

Despite the pressure of having powerful in-laws, Diana was a forceful as well as loving mother, dismissing a royal nanny she did not like, and taking Harry on his first official tour when he was only one.

The Queen at Epsom Derby

It is said that the queen is at her happiest around horses. In the 1950s she was twice nominated 'British flat racing Championship owner' though a victory in the Epsom Derby (pictured, 1988) has eluded her. In June 2013 she celebrated the triumph of her horse, 'Estimate', at the Gold Cup at Royal Ascot, the first reigning monarch's horse to win in its two-hundred-year history.

Beside her is her cousin, Prince Michael of Kent (also a grandson of George V), who has a strong resemblance to the last Russian Tsar. He is a celebrity in Russia and was invited to attend the formal burial of Nicholas II in Saint Petersburg in 1998 – his DNA had helped identify the Tsar's remains in 1979.

The Queen Mother's Birthday

For many, the Queen Mother was a national grandmother figure who never seemed to age. Fondly known for her love of gin and horseracing (although she never bet), and her rapport with people, she stunned the Shah of Iran's advisers and courtiers by talking to people of all social classes while on a visit there. This photograph of her family, taken outside her home at Clarence House, includes her daughter Elizabeth's youngest son, some sixty-three years her junior.

The Queen Mother's ninetieth birthday, a year later than this photograph, was marked by a parade in London involving the three hundred organisations she had worked with down the years. Five years later she attended commemorations for the fiftieth anniversary of the end of the war in which she had done so much to boost the people's morale, despite having had two major operations that year, one on her eye and the other on her hip. Her hundredth birthday was celebrated by performances and speeches from ninety-year-old actor Sir John Mills and eighty-five-year-old comedian Norman Wisdom. After the age of 101, she had a major fall but insisted on standing for the national anthem during a memorial service for her husband sixty years after his death, soon after her daughter Margaret (a smoker like her father) had died. The Queen Mother passed away the following month.

The Royal Cousins

In 1986 Andrew married Sarah Ferguson, who, like Diana, was a descendant of one of Charles II's numerous mistresses (more curiously, the Duchess of Kent is a descendant of Oliver Cromwell – and a Catholic) and the daughter of a major who was also Charles's polo teacher.

Although initially praised for her informality, 'Fergie' had all of Diana's problems with the press with little of the latter's charm, and the British public eventually became hostile. From the ill-fated royal 'It's A Knock-Out' television programme to indecent pictures with her financial advisers, and later accusations of using her royal connections for profit, scandal has never been far away. Yet for a time the couple were happy, and produced two daughters, Beatrice in 1988 and Eugenie two years later.

Although the couple split in 1996, their divorce was unusually amicable, they shared parenting happily and remained friends (indeed Andrew has found himself in trouble for trying to help out his ex-wife financially), and they lived together from 2008 after her house burned down. Although three of the queen's children's marriages had failed, Andrew and Fergie did prove to be model divorcees. Both Beatrice (pictured here with cousin Harry holding hands) and Eugenie (in her mother's arms) have become more active in royal duties in recent years.

Diana at the Taj Mahal

The photograph of Diana sitting down outside the Taj Mahal – the beauty and grandeur of the palace making her loneliness all the more stark – illustrated the decline of the couple's marriage perhaps more than any other. What made it all the more poignant was that this 'jewel of Muslim art in India' is a great monument to romantic love, built by Shah Jajan in 1631 in tribute to his wife Mumtaz (just as London's Charing Cross was originally one of twelve Eleanor Crosses built by Edward I in memory of his wife in 1291–4).

Rumours had been circulating for some time, but Andrew Morton's book *Diana, Her True Story*, published in June 1992, was a sensation. When the royal couple's separation was announced by Prime Minister John Major in December, in front of a packed House of Commons, *The New York Times* described it as an 'unhappy ending … to a storybook marriage gone badly wrong'.

They divorced in 1996 and Diana lost her title – although William had apparently pledged to give it back to his 'mummy' – but she certainly retained many people's sympathy.

Windsor Castle Fire

The year 1992 became known as the *annus horribilis*, a phrase the queen popularised at a speech to the Guildhall in November. In March it was announced that Andrew and Sarah Ferguson were to separate, and the following month Anne and Captain Mark Phillips divorced, while Charles and Diana's marriage was very publicly falling apart.

To top it all off, Windsor Castle caught fire in November and there was little sympathy for the prime minister's suggestion that taxpayers pick up the bill, the castle being government-owned. Such was the public outcry – during the depths of a recession – that a solution was reached whereby the costs would be covered by opening the palaces to tourism.

Then, in December, it was announced that Charles and Diana would separate – this Windsor family Christmas cannot have been fun. There were also recordings in which both parties were caught speaking to their lovers. The nadir for the family came in 1995, when Diana was interviewed by Martin Bashir for the BBC's 'Panorama' programme in which, noticeably wide-eyed and teary, she said there were 'three people' in her marriage (the other being Charles's girlfriend, Camilla Parker-Bowles) and that she would like to be 'a queen of people's hearts', catchphrases which became part of the national vocabulary.

Diana's Campaign Against Landmines

Diana's charity work, always important to her, became more so after her marriage ended. As well as Great Ormond Street Hospital, she remained involved with the homeless charity, Centrepoint, the Leprosy Mission, National Aids Trust and the Royal Marsden Hospital.

Perhaps most famously, and controversially, she became active in the campaign against landmines, and the picture of her standing by a minefield in Angola is one of many of the princess which is instantly recognisable, copied and spoofed. During her last summer she spoke at conferences in London, Washington and Bosnia about landmines, and while in the United States she met Mother Teresa (who was to die just three days after her) in the Bronx.

The worldwide ban on landmines was perhaps her greatest legacy. Just four months after her death 161 states signed the Ottawa Treaty banning their use, and her campaigning had a big influence. When the Second Reading of the Landmines Bill took place in 1998, Foreign Secretary Robin Cook paid tribute to Diana and 'the immense contribution' she had made.

Her last official engagement in England before her death in August 1997 was at a children's accident and emergency unit in London.

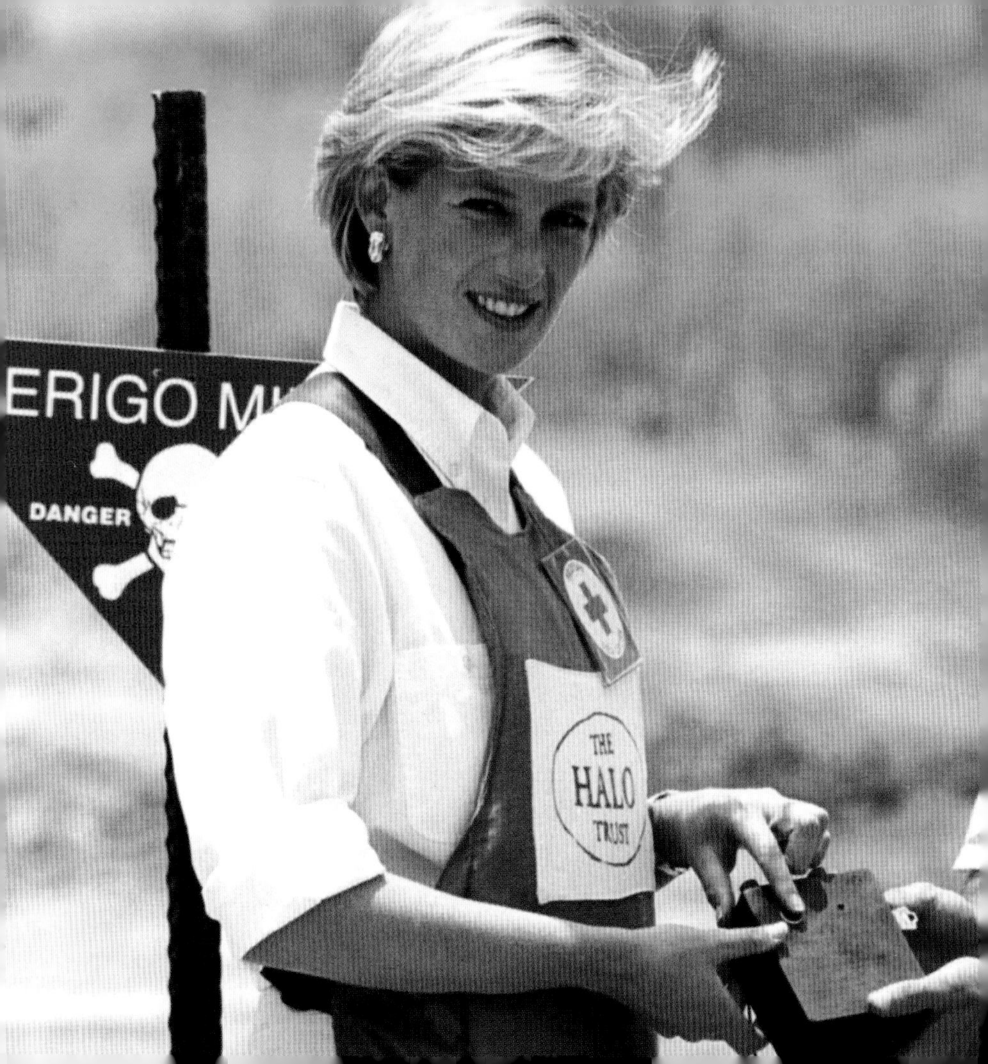
ERIGO M
DANGER
THE HALO TRUST

Diana's Funeral

The sight of the young Harry behind the coffin of his mother was the most poignant moment of an extraordinary week of public mourning following Diana's death in August 1997.

The reserved and stoical royal family, already unpopular because of their treatment of the princess, was forced by a Buckingham Palace crowd to come and display their grief, and to change protocol by flying the flag at half-mast. A moment of great cultural and historical importance, it was later portrayed in a movie, *The Queen* (2006), with Helen Mirren in the starring role.

Although blame for Diana's death in a Paris underpass had rested with Dodi Fayed's drunken driver, Henri Paul, and the paparazzi pursuing their car – at the funeral her brother Charles, Earl Spencer (left), reflected that Diana, named after the goddess of hunting, had become the most hunted person on earth – there was a great deal of anger directed at the royal family too. Diana had been just a girl when she had married a much older more powerful man, and was seen as the victimised underdog. There was also a sense that the public themselves (and their voracious appetite for royal gossip) shared some of the blame. This image shows Harry, William and their father with Diana's brother.

Charles, William and Harry

The royal family has often gone through popularity cycles – Queen Victoria was hugely detested in the 1870s, yet by the time of her jubilee in 1897 she was a much-loved figure of British pride. But the return of the Windsors after their 1990s traumas was astonishing, although it has not been entirely accidental, 'the Firm' having paid handsomely for top public-relations experts. In their favour, there was by now public unease at the intrusion of the press, and a widespread feeling that Diana's boys should not be a circus act.

The British press even reverted to the old-fashioned gentlemen's agreements, so that when William went to St Andrew's University, newspapers largely kept their distance, and sneaky shots of Prince William's wife, published in foreign media in 2012, would be rejected by British tabloids, with the support of their readers.

The quid pro quo was that the press would receive occasional photos of the royals, who will always continue to fascinate the public, including family photos such as this warm image of Charles and his sons. Although Charles did not have the natural empathy of his former wife, there is no doubting the genuinely close relationship he has with his sons.

Marriage of Charles and Camilla

Despite some misgivings – a couple of protesters in the crowd outside declared that he was unfit to be king – Charles and Camilla had their happy ever after. While millions lined the streets for his first wedding, his second featured just close family invited to a civil ceremony in Windsor, followed by a religious blessing, Charles's parents attending only the latter. The marriage was even delayed twenty-four hours so that Charles could attend the funeral of Pope John Paul II.

Charles's own divorce was not the problem for the Church of England that he will one day lead, as his first wife was dead, but Camilla's husband wasn't, and so it was agreed that a civil service was the best option. This threw up obscure legal questions in itself, as royals were specifically excluded from the 1836 act creating civil marriages, and although eleven 'concerned' citizens objected to the marriage on these grounds, the registrar ruled that the 1998 Human Rights Act overruled it.

Despite the late Diana's heartbreak at there being three in her marriage, the extended Windsor-Parker-Bowles family got on well. After the guests were brought along in a royal minibus, Prince William and Tom Parker-Bowles acted as witnesses.

Soldier Harry Being Inspected by the Queen

After the death of his mother, the Army proved Prince Harry's making and his surrogate family. Nicknamed 'Ugly' by his comrades in the Blues and Royals, 'Harry Wales' is known to enjoy the camaraderie of the armed forces, and its levelling effect – officers and men alike enduring the soldier's lot. He served on the front line in Afghanistan, flying helicopter missions and firing weapons in direct combat with the Taliban, until (much to his frustration) an Australian newspaper broke his cover.

Harry has had the odd slip, photographed occasionally in states of inebriation, wearing inappropriate fancy dress or nothing at all. Despite, or because of this, he remains popular with a British public who not only sympathise with the loss he has suffered and the stress of being under the spotlight, but have a great deal of respect for soldiers of the armed forces, alongside the royal family still a revered British institution in the early twenty-first century.

Harry did not thrive academically, but he showed aptitude at sport and the qualities necessary for the life of an officer, and while his brother settled into university life, the military academy at Sandhurst always seemed the natural option for Harry. Although William looks far more like their mother, the younger son has inherited her charitable interests, and after school went to Lesotho to help with Aids victims.

William and Kate Just Wed

Given space from media intrusion after his mother's death, William studied at St Andrew's (the university saw a leap in female applications the following year), where he met his future wife, Catherine (Kate) Middleton. Middleton, the daughter of two British Airways workers who went on to start their own multi-million pound business, represented a new dynamic in the history of the royal family – their marriage into the wider middle class. Famously, William had first met her while she was taking part in a fashion shoot, and she had persuaded him to stay on at university when he was homesick.

William proposed in October 2010, with the wedding held in April the following year, thirty years after his parents' marriage, and the enthusiasm of the day surprised even cynics. As well as a million people lining the streets, there was a peak live television audience of 26.3 million, highly unusual in the digital age, and some 72 million watched live on the royal family's YouTube channel, as well as keeping up on Twitter and Facebook, a sign of how technology has changed but public fascination with the Windsors remains timeless. There were five thousand street parties to celebrate the young couple, who drove away in Charles's Aston Martin.

William, Kate and Baby George

Having inherited his mother's looks and charm (and height – at 6 feet 3 inches he towers over recent monarchs), Prince William has taken the lead in reviving the family's fortunes as it continues to thrive in yet another century. Perhaps it was that the royals provided a focus of unity in a more fractured nation, or that, unlike with his parents, this was a real love match between two young people, but a century after Edward VII's death, the royal family's popularity had reached a new peak. Much had changed in the century since the death of Edward VII and his son's rebranding of the monarchy, and it has continued to adapt; following the announcement that the Duchess of Cambridge was pregnant, the government announced that boys would no longer take preference in the succession over older sisters, while laws barring Catholics from marrying the heir to the throne would be reversed, showing once again the institution's ability to adapt to changing social mores.

When, on a hot summer's day, Buckingham Palace announced the birth of a son, Prince George Alexander Louis, named after his great-grandfather George VI (and perhaps that monarch's father), it marked the opening of a new chapter in the still-unfinished story of the House of Windsor.

Acknowledgements

Every attempt has been made by the Publishers to secure the appropriate permissions for materials reproduced in this book. If there has been any oversight we will be happy to rectify the situation and a written submission should be made to the Publishers.
All pictures © MirrorPix.

INDEX